NOAH E. BROOKS

NOAH E. BROOKS

Printed in the United States of America

Copyright @ 2023 Noah Emmanuel Brooks
ISBN: ISBN: 9798393721749

Edited by: Synergy Consulting

Cover Design & Book Illustrations: Illustrator- Vladimir Cebu, LL.B.

Book Composed By: Author Sharonette Smart

Book Layout: SHERO Publishing
Greenlight Creations Graphics Designs
www.glightcreations.com

Published by: SHERO Publishing

SHEROPublishing.com
ericaperrygreen@gmail.com

Library of Congress Cataloging-in-Publication Data

Noah's Village Reads

DEDICATION

Noah's Village Reads is a non-profit organization dedicated to the literacy advancement and enrichment of our future generations. The literary collection of NVRS books are developed to teach life lessons that reinforces manners, morals and ethical values.

At NVRS we know that "Knowledge is available when reading is applied." The first series of NVRS collection focuses on the importance of using our manners. Creating a foundation from which to grow is the goal of this series.

Noah Emmanuel Brooks is the author and inspiration for NVRS.

"Knowledge is available, when reading is applied."

2

GG loves Noah so much. She misses the days when Noah was an infant, a toddler, and he depended on her and his mommy for everything. While GG is glad to see Noah growing big and strong, she's not sure how she feels about this independent stage he's going through.

"Good morning, Noah, it's time to brush your teeth." GG takes out the toothbrush and his strawberry-flavored toothpaste. GG puts the toothpaste on the toothbrush and proceeds to brush Noah's teeth. Noah refuses to open his mouth.

"I can do it myself!" says Noah. As he grabs the toothbrush and puts it in his mouth. His independence and determination left most of the toothpaste on the sink and counter, instead of in his mouth. "Noah, if only you had let me help you, this would not have happened." Said GG.

GG walks into Noah's room and says, "Okay Noah, it's time to get dressed. We have a long day today. Let me help you put on your clothes." "I'm not a baby GG! I can do it MYSELF!" says Noah.

"I know you can Noah, but there is nothing wrong with you letting me help you," replies GG. Determined to do it himself, Noah struggled to get himself dressed, without any help from GG.

8

"It will be chilly today, Noah, let me help you put on your coat, hat, gloves and scarf." GG says.

"I can do it MYSELF!" Noah replies, as he struggles to get his coat on and zipped up. After three attempts, Noah finally gets it zipped!

Excited to see what he has accomplished, Noah turns to GG and says, "See GG, I told you, I can do it MYSELF!"

GG tries to help Noah put on his hat and scarf, but he quickly replies, "I got it GG!" "I CAN DO IT MYSELF!"

10

GG unlocked the car and attempted to assist Noah in locking himself in his car seat.

"I can do it **MYSELF!**" said Noah.
He locked himself in the car seat. While Noah was well able of doing so, GG explained, "Noah, I must check it to make sure that you did a good job, okay Noah?

"Okay GG, but I did it **MYSELF!**" Noah replied. "Great job!" GG exclaimed.

GG and Noah arrived at Noah's school. Noah unlocked his car seat and got out of the car. He was excited about school. GG went to input the code to enter his school when Noah passionately explained to GG that it was his school, and he could login himself!

By this time GG is exhausted with the *Independent Noah*. Later that afternoon, when GG picked Noah up from school, she told Noah that she had a surprise for him. GG announced that they were going out to have pasta for dinner! Noah loves spaghetti!

When they arrived at the restaurant, GG warned Noah to be on his best behavior inside.

13

When the spaghetti arrived, Noah was hungry, excited, and ready to eat!

GG said, "Let me help you Noah, before you make a mess."

"I can do it MYSELF!" said Noah. He snatched away from GG and accidentally knocked his whole plate of food onto the floor! Spaghetti and sauce went flying everywhere!

This made GG very upset. Needless to say, dinner was over at this point.

16

Extremely angry at the turn of events, GG began to tell Noah how disappointed she was in him.

Ashamed of his actions, Noah stood up by the dinner table and said something that would turn the entire evening around.

Noah said, "GG, you and God-Mommy taught me that *I am Smart! I am Brave! And I can do anything in the name of Jesus!*" Noah continued, "I'm sorry I made a mess GG, but Noah is a big boy, and I can do it MYSELF!"

18

GG was amazed and astonished at the response Noah gave. She began to feel guilty and realized that Noah had been declaring his affirmations. His God-Mommy taught them to him around the age of two. Noah recited this affirmation daily and grew more and more confident in it as the years passed by.

GG would also make sure Noah recited his affirmation whenever he was with her too. She realized that the affirmation Noah recited daily had become a belief system within him. Noah believes, based on the belief system he's established, that Jesus gave him the ability to do ANYTHING himself!

GG turned to Noah and immediately apologized for getting upset and not allowing Noah to feed himself. She explained that she was only trying to help.

Noah interjects and says, "It's Okay GG, you didn't mean to get upset with me!" GG smiles, and reaffirms Noah, "You are Smart!" "You are Brave!" "And YES, you can do ANYTHING in the name of Jesus!"

"That's right!" says Noah! "Now GG, will you make me some spaghetti when we get home, Noah is hungry?"

With a smile, GG replies, "I sure will. I Love You Noah!"

"I love you too, GG!" Noah replies with a big hug!

THE
END

Dear Parent, Caregiver or Loved One...

It is extremely Important that we help develop and nurture a positive belief system within our children. What we speak over and about our children plays an important role in who they are, who they will become, and what it is that they believe about themselves. Speaking life over our children can make a difference in the human being they grow up to be.

Affirmations are extremely important. Validating and reinforcing those affirmations is our responsibility. The repetition and mouth confession of the affirmation creates a belief system that can't be broken. Take the time to develop your own affirmation for your child, children, grandchildren, or godchildren as God-Mommy did for Noah. If you can't think of one you can always use Noah's!

> **"I Am Smart!**
> **I Am Brave!**
> **And I Can Do ANYTHING In The Name Of Jesus!"**

Death and life is in the power of the tongue. (Proverbs 18:21)
Justified or condemned by your words. (Matthew 12:37)

SPEAK LIFE! Say about your children what God has said about them. *They are fearfully and wonderfully made.* (Psalm 139:14)

Noah's Affirmation

My mouth confession...
I am Noah Emmanuel Brooks.
I am healthy. I am wealthy. And I am wise.
I will never be broke a day in my life.
I am the righteousness of God.
I am the seed of Abraham.
Everything I am, I am because God Is!
And because God Is,
I am Noah Emmanuel Brooks.

They can't hide it in a book,
if we're writing the book.
~NEB

Knowledge is available, when reading is applied ~NVRS

A Few Affirmations That You Can Confess Daily

I AM…

I Am the head and not the tail… Deuteronomy 28:13

I Am above and not beneath… Deuteronomy 28:13

I Am a lender and not a borrower… Deuteronomy 15:6

I Am the light of the world… Matthew 5:14

I Am the salt of the earth… Matthew 5:13

I Am more than a conqueror… Romans 8:37

I Am a new creature… 2 Corinthians 5:17

I Am made in the image and likeness of God... Genesis 1:26

I Am Saved… Romans 10:9

I Am free from all condemnation… Romans 8:1

I Am strong and courageous… Joshua 1:7

I Can Do All Things Through Christ Who Strengthens Me…
Philippians 4:13

About The Author

Author Noah Emmanuel Brooks is currently four years old and attends Primrose School at Brier Creek.

Noah loves sports, attending church, and his family. Noah enjoys singing in the youth church choir at Victorious Praise Fellowship COGIC church. His favorite sports are football and baseball, which he loves playing with his Dad.

With encouragement from his GG, Author Sharonette Smart, Noah is now a two-time published author. His first book entitled, *How Noah Got The Cookie From The Cookie Jar*, also shared strong lessons for both the youth and caregivers. Noah looks forward to being a BIG Brother and BIG Cousin this year!

We look forward to Noah's continued success.

I Can Do It Myself

Noah's Independent Stage

AUTHOR
NOAH E. BROOKS

What are your Affirmations?

_____

_____

_____

_____

_____

_____

_____

_____

What are some of the lessons you learned?

_____

_____

_____

_____

_____

_____

_____

_____

Made in the USA
Columbia, SC
23 May 2023